Paddling the Canoe

Lorraine Haig
Paddling the Canoe

Acknowledgements

Grateful acknowledgement is made to the editors of the following anthologies and journals where some of these poems first appeared: *Poetry d'Amour, Poetry Matters, Australian Poetry Journal, Windfall, Blue Giraffe, Presence* (UK)

Special thanks to Liz Winfield for her assistance
and Robyn Mathison for her encouragement.

I want to acknowledge my husband Tony, who was a patient sounding board, and Kristen Lang for her enthusiastic support.

For my mother Fay
with love and gratitude

Paddling the Canoe
ISBN 978 1 76109 094 3
Copyright © text Lorraine Haig 2021
Cover photo by the author

First published 2021 by
GINNINDERRA PRESS
PO Box 3461 Port Adelaide 5015 Australia
www.ginninderrapress.com.au

Contents

All shapes of love
  Crawling to the light   11
  Life drawing   12
  Up in the blue air   13
  The periphery of memory   15
  The mountain   17
  The small sorrow   18
  Into the unknown   19
  The seed   21
  Through the lens   23
  The worst pain   24
  The world's light fades   25
  Jade   26
  Butterfly   27
  Forgiveness   28
  Painting the canoe   29
  The swift passage of horses   31
  Poetry in glass   32
  If love was a painting   33
  Painting mangos   34
  When lapis lazuli is leaving   35
  More than a star map   36
  The last ride   37
  Fjord   38

Grounded
  Duck egg morning   41
  Old Richmond Road   43
  The river   44
  Southerly   46

Apprehension	48
Among sinuous limbs	49
Three haiku	51
Fish-bone myth	52
Breathless things	54
The scent of pine	55
Noisy miners	57
Bushfire Cinquains	59
The red-bellied black	60
Someone's packing up and leaving	61
The bushman's carnival	62
She photographs the drought	63
Van Gogh paints a starry night in Australia	65
Imagine a city	67
The horse in the jungle	71
The city of sleep	73
Dutch Elm on the Canal du Midi	75
Going to the island	76
Go to Tokyo	78
Minutiae	80

Autumn's Passage

Autumn riot	83
A place called somewhere	84
The music of snow	85
Living in the cracks	86
The journey	88
A lasting memory	89
Dinner for six	90
There's someone else living here	91
Combined Assets and Income Assessment	92
Small poems of loss for my mother	94

Weaving life into a day	95
Looking after chickens	96
A splinter of light	98
The dark disturbance	99
The egret on the edge	100
Above the lake	101
About the author	102

All shapes of love

gathering
all the colours of morning
wattlebird's song.

All shapes of love is from a quote by Arthur Rimbaud

Crawling to the light

A poem is a toddler taking its first steps.
A poem can seep into every cell of your body.
A poem is made from memory and magic;
        it names impossible things.
A poem cannot hibernate; it must crawl from the cave,
        breathe fresh air and fill its belly.
A poem is a portion of heart and mind, ventricles
        woven into flesh.
You can dance between lines and hold the words tight.
A poem can dive deep into darkness or float,
        colour emerging from the depths.
You're allowed to fend it off or let it swim inside.
There is no holding back when a wave of emotion
        drags you out clinging to a raft of words.
A poem is there in front of you with its dressing gown
        wide open.
It belongs to everyone when released.
A poem is something that can fly over you
        or fly into you.
It uses feline charms.
It negotiates a city, no hands on the wheel.
It is a jigsaw, pieces missing so you can add your own.
A poem is a way to warm you – sip its words slowly.
A poem is made from patches of life's fabric.
A poem is a quilt to wrap around your shoulders
        when there's nothing else.
It is brave. It can stand in the ring, fists ready.
It's to share yourself and know
        someone will carry you in their heart.

Life drawing

I focus on high cheekbones.
Caught in the glare of a powerful globe
the chiaroscuro of muscle and bone.
Unlike the cool stare of Manet's Olympia,
he doesn't meet our gaze.
How self-possessed he seems
under eight pairs of eyes, how flexible
holding one-minute poses
enough for us to gain hand-eye coordination.
Then five minutes twisting and bending.
As he positions himself in the stream of light,
our efforts to capture form are clumsy.
We break and he (towel around hips)
peruses our efforts, remains silent.

The cold hovers over the stall where he sells:
>Birds; their black necks made from chains;
>cars and bikes from nuts and bolts,
>soft drink cans cut and shaped – stuff
>others would throw away.

He's aware of the crowd, but he's alone.
I may be the only one watching who knows
that on his right buttock is tattooed
a winged creature flying from the light.

Up in the blue air

A god of sun and surf
he stood before her; half her world,
dripping light. The sea runs down his body,
ocean-blue eyes.
Come on he says to his two-year-old.
They walk into the waves.
Holding her
he ignores her whimpers, wades deeper.
Straddling his neck
she clings to his ears.
Up in the blue air, invisible hands
grip her ankles,
vanish under hissing foam.
Her screams disappear
beneath the waves.
Alone in the ocean,
here is love – a terrified child,
the first taste of abandonment
on her father's shoulders.

On my father's shoulders
the first taste of abandonment.
Here is love, a terrified child
alone in the ocean.
Beneath the waves
my screams disappear,
vanish under hissing foam.
Gripping my ankles,
up in the blue air, invisible hands.
I cling to his ears,
straddling his neck.
He ignores my whimpers, wades deeper.
Holding me,
we walk into the waves.
Come on he says to his two-year-old.
Ocean-blue eyes
dripping light. The sea runs down his body.
He stood before me, half my world,
a god of sun and surf.

The periphery of memory

1.

I told you to stop running inside the tent.
At three years of age I backed away from my cousin
into a frying pan. Screams drown the sound
of the ocean. I've lost my memory
of the pain but I still have the disobedient scars.

2.

Sucking on liquorice cigarettes at the movies
behind the boy with sun-bleached hair,
the one I had a crush on.
I should have blown love darts,
pierced his skin. Made him notice
the dark eyes, the shy smile surrounding
stained, black teeth.

3.

There was a heatwave
the summer I finally found the courage
to leave a house full to overflowing
with disappointment.
Each day sizzled – so hot I could taste it.
The nearest bus one hundred kilometres
over a goat track scattered with peppercorn trees.

4.

That place called somewhere
is just out of reach in my mother's mind.
It's where galahs brim with laughter
as they swing upside-down from the wires
and where a flock of cockatoos
is spread like a white sheet over the trees.
The hum of a tractor   fades
beneath a ploughed sky.

The mountain

I'm so sorry darling
his last words,
as they skidded
in front of the oncoming traffic,
colliding with a vehicle, before they plunged.
Her airbag inflated,
punched its fist in her face,
knocked her out. The car hurtled
down the mountainside
on its roof, trees flying past either side.
She woke
to the bash and grind of rocks and scrub
tearing at the car
as it slid like a toboggan,
its descent halted by a big gum.
She remembers the silence
after the terrible noise –
then the smell of petrol.
The driver's seat had gone. One of his shoes
was still there. Her face hurt.
She searched for the seat belt clip.
Fell on her head into glass.
The door wouldn't open.
She screamed, clawed the window.
Then strong hands
hauled her into fresh air
and the mist
that was rolling over them,
rolling on down the mountain.

The small sorrow

In the old photo you look up to the camera
from where you sit on a camping stool,

a joey in your lap. Your mouth is open,
but your words are a lost conversation.

Your dark eyes, like the joey's eyes,
look gentle, vulnerable. Her small, grey head,

her long eyelashes protrude from a blanket –
a substitute for her mother's warm pouch.

You hold a plastic dolly's bottle
and you're about to feed this small sorrow.

But what can't be seen
is the broken tail, the bone severed midway

by the bullet you fired from the 303 towards
the long twitching ears in the spinifex.

Into the unknown

You step into a deep, dark hole
when told your child
will not develop
past the age of 12.

You cope by taking one day at a time;
attend occupational, speech
and physiotherapy,
but you wonder whether it will make
a damn bit of difference.

There you are; you, your one-year-old daughter
and your partner, whom you rarely see now
because he copes by fishing.
You step on the time travelator towards 12.
That big, black number,
now the future, is a terminal illness.

12 is still below the horizon
when your daughter sits for the first time
without toppling sideways. At three years of age
she stands taking her first, stiff steps.
There are nine years to go.

12 is looming larger. It rises each morning
like a full eclipse. She starts school and the bullies
circle her like wolves.

In her tenth year you make a chocolate cake together
and it wins a prize at the local show.
As the shadow of the giant 12 darkens the grass
the three of you sit in the sun. You're beginning to hope
the towering 12 is only made of cardboard.
You stare up as you pass between
the two numerical skyscrapers. It's weathered
while you've weathered eleven years. Your daughter
will start high school in her thirteenth year.

The seed

i

The black cockatoos squawk
a change in weather.

I look under stones. Search for release.
There's nothing there.
Nothing but a scrap of fur,
a few seeds. Overhead
the tops of trees tear the sky.
The air filters the screaming.
Wide trunks listen
on the cold side of their faces.

The dirt road winds uphill, the colour of flesh,
the colour of my padded coat.
Hunker down in the spiky grass.
Open my backpack,
pull out my drawing book, charcoal,
a thermos – pour tea, taste stone-cold disbelief.
Images on the page smear.

In my temple
of trees, whatever's been stalking
has moved inside.
It blew in from under the rock
(not the scrap of fur)
down a warm, moist corridor,
the seed lodging under my ribs.
Tenacious.
Growing conditions perfect.

ii

Cliff-high, there's lightness in my bones.
If I climb
over and over
will I fly?
The seagull hovers
eyeing my lunch. Does he want me
to join him?
Such blueness.
Sky and ocean stitch themselves.
I draw your face; fold you into a paper plane.
Why is it so hard to let go?

iii

When the news came
by telephone of her death,
there was a terrible wailing
as I stared out the window
at the houses
on the far hill and wondered why,
with such a view,
their windows were so small.

Through the lens

After 'Sounding the name' by Robert Kroetsh

In this poem my daughter is not dead.
She is in the backyard,
on an old chair, her blonde curls cascading
around her face, her hand cupping pellets
for the white chicken in her lap.

In this poem she looks towards the camera,
her eyes and her head
yet to turn slightly to the right as a red-headed boy
saunters into view, smiling at her, two years
before he smiles like that at another girl.

In this poem my daughter is not dead.
The phone does not ring
that June morning of her nineteenth year,
the estranged voice delivering the news
in a shockingly ordinary tone.

The worst pain

Back then he ruled her life,
even told her when to breathe.
His anger was red and deep.

Twice she left home. The first time
he wore her down. The next time
she packed all her belongings
in a few boxes.
Left her marriage, the snake
that bailed her up,
the people she knew,
fish, salted and drying
on the clothesline and life
became kinder.

After the death of your child
living is the hardest thing you can do.
The pain is so intense
you can't touch it.
A small voice says, do it now!
To fall asleep without pills, lie there,
meditate on your breathing.
Will you live
as long as your mother?

When she sleeps, her inner most thoughts
are on the inside of her eyelids.
She is the only one she confides in.

Her name means
        move through life unseen.

The world's light fades

It might be the blue tongue sunning on the deck
or the ginger cat that glances back
as it sneaks down the path into the bushes,
or the blackbird on the railing that witnesses
the moment the world's light fades
from my eyes on the seventeenth of May,
two weeks before my birthday.

I am choosing that day because
it is my sister's birthday. I am choosing her birthday
because she died on mine.
There is no maliciousness in my decision. I want
to bind us in death as we were not bound in life.
It will be on a Wednesday like today and I will be alone.
It will be raining. It must be raining as I don't want
my shadow to witness my death.

Lorraine is dead. She died dripping wet
in a dash from the shower,
the phone call transferred to message bank
while the yellow-tailed cockatoos
screeched overhead, predicting rain.

Jade

There is, *if only*, the barbed taunt of hindsight
sharp as the metallic tongues of blackbirds.
There are regrets jading the edge of memory
like candlelight flickering in the eye's corner.

There's a fading photograph of her that blurs reality
and beginnings surface out of grief. There is
a jade necklace that hints of her skin and her jade
elephant, its green lustre luminous in the sun.

After twenty years, the grief and the guilt
have worn smooth, my memories of her
are jade – glazed and polished, gems
preserved in the brain's fastidious store.

Butterfly

Tremulous, I wake each morning
as the sun streams in.

I thrill to the warmth of light
as I flutter between sleep and dream.

You stretch out for me across a meadow
and barely feel my ripple on your fingers.

Try as I might I cannot see beyond
each moment drifting across my skin.

Forgiveness

We could sit in the sunshine
and tell stories of tree climbing
and the reason clouds form animals
or the freedom of pushbikes
and a tanned skin in summer.

We could forget the anger
in the brown eyes, the hazel ones
gloating, and imagine time
vanishing behind the sand hills
or two girls riding a wave in a canoe.

We could let an open window
gather the sounds of night
and spread them over us
like a silk sheet or over the ghosts
wandering the path of childhood.

We could connect the land
over a gaping chasm,
meet in the middle
and fall
into the hug of an only sister.

Painting the canoe

Sometime in 1962 Dad chases me with the broom
for giving cheek. Gosh he can run fast. He catches me
behind the pool and wallops my legs with the handle.
Dad says don't do it again.

Sometime in 1955 Mum walks me to school
on my first day. I wait until she disappears
around the corner. Follow her home.

Sometime in 1967 Dad asks me to pose nude
for his life drawing class. He is serious.

Sometime in 1964 Dad builds a canoe. I pester him
to be allowed to help. I'm given a paint brush
and a tin of pale blue. I squeeze like a contortionist
into the bow, nearly suffocate on the fumes.
Dad says don't spill any.

Sometime in 1975 I paint a picture of Mum in her jeans,
a green jumper around her shoulders. Her red hair
has caught the sun. She is smiling at someone
outside the picture.

Sometime in 1966 after a fight with my sister
I scream I'm going to kill myself. She runs
and tells my parents. Dad yells at me not to be so stupid.

Sometime in 1972 I give birth to a daughter.
The doctor says *see you again next year.*

Sometime in 1960 at Pebbly beach, a cow wanders
into our tent and eats the cornflakes, box and all.

Sometime in 1978 my youngest brother has an eagle
tattooed across his back, the wings fan down his arms.
Dad is furious.

Sometime in 1953 my mother encourages me to play
on the swings. I disobey, line up
with the other children outside the ice cream parlour.
That was the year my sister was born
and I was no longer the centre of my father's eyes.

Sometime in 1982 we move to an island.
Our daughter goes to school on a speedboat.

Sometime in 1968 my friend and I go paddling
on the lake in the canoe. A strong wind comes up.
We start screaming as the waves drench us.
A police boat pulls alongside.

Sometime in 1963 when President Kennedy is shot
I'm in my bedroom making a marionette.

Sometime in 1965 Dad carries the canoe on his shoulders
from the tent to the beach. We laugh as all we can see
is the canoe crawling over sandhills.
Dad says never again.

The swift passage of horses

My life is speeding up –
I swirl through the years
like a spoonful of sugar
stirred into hot tea.

Stir faster
and a vortex appears.
If I'm not careful
I'll be sucked in and disappear.

My father spun honey
into his tea –
though it was more of a gallop.
I always imagined horses.

I tried to emulate
but with my clumsy canter
I only managed to slosh tea
into the saucer.

Dying at sixty-two,
he never reached my age.
Probably never heard the horses
as he propelled his tea.

Poetry in glass

for Émile Gallé

Butterflies, their pale wings,
gather the light, shimmer
on the curve of a concave shell.
Luminescing on a plinth, this bowl
shows perfect poise.

Butterflies in a sky of lemon swarm,
spiralling the glass
in an endless chase. But what if
after one hundred years
they took flight, left the darkness
and shadows of the museum.

Butterflies. Imagine, soft thoraxes
quivering on the open window ledge,
wings spread to sponge the pure light
under their first blue sky dome.

Would the smallest gesture of kindness
coax them to stay?

If love was a painting

If love was a Van Gogh
I'd want to touch its skin
to feel the ridges of the paint
and drink the colours in.

If I wanted to love danger
it's a Caravaggio
how I'd love to be adrift
in the darkness of its shadow.

If love was a Vermeer
it would be my addiction
in a room of light and nuance
left guessing its intention.

If my days seemed a confusion
my dreams an empty echo
If I had a melancholy perspective
I'd be in love with a de Chirico.

If love was a Matisse
I'd be out *en plein air*
lying naked in the sun
yellow daisies in my hair.

If I loved a wild imagination
painted terrors in the void
tormented figures in a landscape
it would be an Arthur Boyd.

Painting mangos

A dish of mangos on a chair in the garden
firm fleshed, blushed by the sun
they've the scent of summer's pleasure
juicy gold in a bowl of sky-blue

the primed canvas seems to shimmer
for the touch of his brush on its skin
ripe to paint before the light changes
he's watching his wife peeling fruit

she curves at the sink slurping peaches
wipes the juice as it runs from her chin
in this heat her movements are languid
and he shivers with a yearning fire

dark hair swept up from her shoulders
he's wishing she'd pose on the grass
so he could paint the flame – not of mangos
but the craving he hoards in his hands.

When lapis lazuli is leaving

Roll around your mouth
a sound so deliciously foreign.

The large L, tongue resting behind the top teeth
followed by the breathy A exhaled around

the side of the tongue. The lips meeting
on the precipice of P puffing the air in a short burst.

Ignoring the I sandwiched between a puff and hiss of
consonants, the S whistles like sand in the desert
snaking around the teeth.

Expelled from the warm cave LAZ resonates
where darkness hides its throaty growl. U pouts a kiss
before LI leaves on the flick of a tongue.

More than a star map

Her life-poem begins to shape itself
as the mermaid emerges.
Leaving her sunglasses on the surface
she discovers a hidden world.

In the saloon a dish of needles
sits next to a green bowl of twine.
How easily he reels her in
though she can't pierce his pain.

Their small ship navigates by a star map
exploring inaccessible places.
They've seen the skeletons of whales
and coined thirty words for clouds.

Now it's a floating classroom
where her sons lengthen hours
listening to the radio, asking questions
about a lack of rainfall, hard winter frosts.

The boys discuss bushfires –
brilliant colour they see in sunsets.
They know little of the land, dwelling
in the cool spectrum of a fluid world.

The last ride

In a furious sea, thick kelp
        smooth as sea lions
                rides the crests.

A muscly undercurrent
        tows it back.
                It's the rope in a tug o' war
        between wind and tide.

Whipped up wave-tops
        jet seaward
                leaving the kelp
        encased in a jade membrane.

Soon it rides its last wave
        to be served up like folds
                of freshly cooked pasta
on a white plate.

Fjord

Let
me
shimmy
up the side of the
mountain; eat soft, clean snow, sit on
the white precipice between the blue sky and grey sea.
I want to watch the red ship pass by the bright cabins
at the water's edge, the bow wave
rippling memories
of life
in
boats.

Grounded

lifting
the whole tree
white cockatoos

Duck egg morning

A lemon light
slices through the arch, and you
walking alongside the river
relish the quiet moments
with yourself and a few
disinterested ducks.
You stop, have time to notice
the sun
how it rims
the crusty edge of sandstone,
splays over reeds
clustered at the river's edge.
The morning, so new, so unrelenting
is for you as fresh
as a shower of rain –
make of it what you will, some might say,
surprising as the duck's egg
laid on dewy grass, still warm,
now cradled in your palm –
its mottled, blue-grey sheen
is something like an old bruise,
or perhaps dimpled cloud
belonging to another morning
that lowered the sky,
crumpled your mood.

You break the small sun
into a blue dish
slide it into batter
where, when stirred, transforms
the whiteness gold.
It stirs the trace of a memory
too deep to surface
and your eyes travel
to the fish pond
just beyond the window
and you remember
you forgot to sprinkle flakes
to the hungry shoal.
The trickle
of water into water,
something like the liquid resonance
of the butcherbird's song,
now silent as the bird turns
a pernicious eye to the pond
thinking perhaps
of a meal, then flies away.
Small bubbles ring the pancakes
before they're flipped,
then slid from the pan
to be sprinkled
with sugar and lemon juice.

Old Richmond Road

I loved the way the narrow road
puttered around the paddocks like an old car
as if there were no hurry.
The way it skirted the corner through a grove
that in autumn flirted gold and orange.
And the way it reached the top of the hill
near the dairy, where each morning
traffic stopped for the herd of Friesians,
udders swinging as they ambled
towards their paddock.
I loved the way my eyes kept darting to the view
of the bay that slanted off to the left
leaving small islands pricked with light.

The way it never came close
to the shepherd's hut that still keeps watch,
and the tourists who pulled over
and pulled out cameras.
This winding, bumpy road was there
before the semi-trailers barrelled along,
elbowing traffic onto the shoulder.
Long before the wineries had mushroomed
along its length. When tractors and fruit farms
were a way of life and not a nuisance.
The graceful curves are nearly all gone,
and now the road misses the point
of the slow drive to an Edwardian village
and its convict ancestry.

The river

Tidy up after breakfast
tie on sneakers   the sky a blue
I've seen in Venice that in turn
reminded me of autumn
on this island
edging the Southern ocean.
I stretch into a pace too fast
eager to be out.
The road curves past a writer's house. A man
who won The Miles Franklin Award   twice.
Did he sit at a desk
above the river that cascades over a weir
wanders into smeared light
before it spreads
into the bay   a depth
now too shallow
for the ships that once sailed there.
I walk the plank
across a grassy bog
spook a cloud of goldfinches
in long grass
gold and crimson
flicker like confetti in an updraught.
Under the shadow of Butcher's Hills
a new house rises   dark brick
a stark contrast
to the sandstone scarp
and the narrative; convicts who
cut blocks and loaded handcarts
under an overseer's cruel eye.

Near the old church mothers chat
after dropping their kids off at school.
A narrow track winds into the old graveyard
a movie surfaces
in my mind   drags me
into a dark night   headstones askew
thunder   lightning   open coffins.
I walk past shiny granite
fresh earth
pressed with flowers.
Head-high reeds rustle
their seed heads. Though I've a fear of snakes
it's the rattlesnake I hear;
one we don't have.
A pademelon moves deeper into stalks.
A gurgle subdues the rattle as I near the river –
here just a shallow trickle. I cross
climb the other bank   stepping over
a half-eaten rat.
Red eye   pale yellow beak –
a startled swamp hen flees.
I follow a dirt track
along the river's edge to where
tourists take photos of the old bridge
smiling faces
where that overseer   sleeping on the parapet
fell   or was pushed
into the dark river.

Southerly

The southerly arrives from the Southern Ocean.
It's ravaged Antarctica, raced over raging seas
to deposit itself in a coastal city.
Is it responsible for the barren hills
sucked of moisture along the river's mouth?
Chimneys exhale into it, people huddle
inside, shut doors to shut it out.

Many a tourist has been caught,
rushing to buy warm clothes
or to arrive at the airport
in flimsy tank tops and sandals
when the locals, there to meet someone,
are rugged in fleecy outdoor gear.

Soup is hauled from the freezer, defrosted,
snow falls
on the mountain,
visitors are goggle-eyed in wonder,
the rest of the country is gadding about
in shorts and thongs.

It reminds us
what little control we really have
as we drag extra blankets from the cupboards.
It's common to hear *four seasons in one day.*
There's always a warm jacket in the car boot.

Hail ricochets off the roof.
and piles up at the window –
small stuff like coarse gravel.
The goldfish hide.
The front can disappear
or return in repeated bursts of fury
punctuated by glorious interludes of light.

The southerly moves on
heads for Sydney
to hassle the yachts and drum up excitement
or foreboding before the big race.

Apprehension

Its sticky tongue laps termites
and ants like milk,
electroreceptors
in the tip of its snout
detecting each morsel
as it gorges across the passage
of a damp night.
Digging in darkness,
criss-crossing memory and scent,
peeling back the surface
to make mince of earth.

In the morning it is gone,
curled under a log or tucked in
for the day beneath bushes.
Miniature bomb craters
scar the garden
and inside each one
there's the shape;
the echidna's slender snout's
fine impression deep in ochre soil
imprinted over and over.

Among sinuous limbs

It's a warm afternoon,
footprints stencil the sand.
You lounge under a tree on a deckchair
soothed by the greasy smell
wafting from the boathouse takeaway
that carries the memory of childhood holidays.
The long throaty toot of the approaching ferry
is remote, but familiar as
the lonely warning
of a liner in fog.
A father steadies his child,
a gesture of love
that lingers
in the splashes of water,
the spade and the red bucket
the boy fills with sand.

A bus roars away from the bus stop.
In the fumes life continues its hectic pace.

A couple, their hamper slung between them
search for shade.
A pelican's deep-throated rumble
tumbles over the river
like an outboard motor   idling
among the sinuous limbs of mangroves,
blue-grey water –
the depth in the eyes of a girl you once knew.

Pelicans gather at the ramp ready to launch
towards the scraps
discarded by fishermen; a flash of fish sliding
down the diaphanous pouch of a bird –
the light reflects off the blade,
blood drips, dissipates.
Boats are winched onto trailers.

The laughter of two four-year-olds
who whiz past on scooters
free, impulsive.
A red jet ski drifts
going nowhere.
Somewhere it is raining hard
nails straight down:
A trip that offers so much spent
under umbrellas, sloshing in streets,
staring out windows into gloomy light.

In the park people make room
for each other
in the barbecue's smoky haze
while above
rainbow lorikeets
squawk and mate among the eucalypts,
clamorous as a thousand grinding train wheels.

Three haiku

mountain track
millipedes moving
towards the sun

                              rock pool
                              a sooty oystercatcher
                              scissors through sky

fading light
bird chatter settles
into frog song

Fish-bone myth

In my garden the dried leaf of *Banksia blechnifolia*
could draw blood. It says stand on me;
I'll pierce your skin.
Its curved ribs, like those of a beached ship's hull
are twisted and broken.
                       Underneath
are tiny dots like spores.
To be ground fine, sprinkled like seed.
On my tongue it's bland and coarse
and tastes of resilience.

Soon it will smell earthy with a faint trace
of the sea. Now dry, it's hard to savour
the odour of creation.

All that is needed is an ancient myth.
> *They say deep in your spine you carry*
> *Gondwana seed.*
> *Sea butterfly,*
> *when the land heaved itself from the ocean,*
> *your blue frills transformed into leaves,*
> *your tail rooted in deep sand.*

If I hold it to my ear I might hear the murmur
of waves or the soft ebb and flow
of kelp forests.

Under a full moon it casts a serrated shadow
or is that the shape
of a fossilised sea creature?

Like my aunt it has curvature of the spine.
It could scratch an itch
or be a contemporary cane chair,
a bespoke design for my aunt. At dawn
it might be a giant centipede
crawling away.
It's a two-edged saw
but not a sawfish skeleton traced
on a shadow board.
Like me it bends before it breaks.

Hidden in the pages of an old book
are the instructions
for growing the fishbone leaf:

> *First take its seed and bury it shallow,*
> *wings protruding. Keep warm and water.*
> *At the first leaf stage, transplant.*

Velvety-bronze foliage will fan out.
Watch in amazement as flowers
shaped like candles spear the air.
When the leaves mature cut one, weave
between three stones and sun-dry.

Breathless things

Today I'm alone, until a raven
descends to the garden.
First I sense its presence – a dark shadow

bends the branch
even before the great weight settles.
The white eye above the sabre-curved beak

surveys my backyard.
I am awed by this messenger
throwing its voice like a black cloak,

drawing out the last *ahhh*; a death rattle
to silence the world.
Sent out to curse the living,

even the wattlebird has vanished.
Condemned to utter that mournful caw
it spills melancholia.

Once death arrives there is no escaping
its strong beak. Breathless things
are carried up to tall trees.

If you look into its white eye, it will know
your inner most secrets and fears
and lament your mortality.

The scent of pine

The dark shadow
that was the pine tree has gone.
Now there's a fence post and pine bark
to mark its passing.
        Gone, the cones that hung
from branches splayed
like ragged wings.
        Gone, the raven
that would perch
on the upper most limbs
to call the wind.
The pine tree was
        chainsawed
and the darkness that was life
        disappeared.
        Now in the distance
there's the old graveyard,
the tall stand of eucalypts,
their pale trunks glistening in the sun.
        The tree has gone,
and the light
that once seeped
through outstretched arms floods in.
The view opens
to the convict gaol,
the pioneer gravestones facing east.

       Now we notice
how the sky
slopes to the dark hills, how it gathers the light
along the rim.
       The trees rise up,
their canopies sweeping clouds.
A yellow tractor mows the ridge,
weaving between the graves.

Noisy miners

She opens the farm gate
and the day unfolds to a warm breeze
and a piercing alarm
that raises
hairs on her arms and vibrates
the fine bones in her ears.
Invisible, up high
in casuarinas and gums
Noisy miners screech
tearing her
away from a thought
that might've expanded to a haiku
were it not for the cacophony
keeping pace along the track.
The birds have punctured
the morning
like the thorny box in the fence
that would prick her skin.
The long, pale grass
strokes her thighs
as she climbs, defenceless
through the slow hour.
When a dam appears,
words like reflection, stillness, peace
sink
below the surface.

She reaches the top
breathes, fills her lungs with silence
and the earthy smell
of sheep beyond the ridge.

Bushfire Cinquains

falling
from a burnt sky
ash the size of hands floats
through an eerie stillness before
the flame

thick smoke
clouds our vision
inhabits the house while
we butter our toast under a
red sun

grant us
a day of rain
heavy if you don't mind
enough to extinguish the fires
dear Lord

thunder
dry lightning stabs
the hills   blows trees apart
makes fire in unreachable
places

bush track…
collect leaves twigs
your greasy fast food trash
build a small mound   it only needs
the match

The red-bellied black

Yesterday, I watched a snake
slither from under the house
and edge towards the long grass;
its dark skin dappled by tree shade.

The next morning I'm outside
riveted to the spot. The snake, a metre away
is galvanised on its tail. Its flicking tongue
surely tastes my fear.

Face to face I am struck
by the hard shine of its underbelly.
Someone once told me
if confronted by a snake stand still.

I obeyed
the fists pounding retreat
in my chest and the voice in my ears
screaming *flee!*

The snake seizes the moment
and vanishes to the undergrowth.
I am filled
with the sweet fragrance

of the frangipani's white flowers
and the pink opal of a snake's belly –
a pale jewel wet and shiny
and my surprise it wasn't red.

Someone's packing up and leaving

Someone always sells the cows,
packs up and moves away.
This town never seems like home.
Summer days top forty-five degrees.
Winter evenings are brittle. The air,
so clear it might crack.

Nights savour the scent of earth
and the sweet pungency of grass.
A town of instant coffee, Akubras
and the crisp exhausts of Holdens.
It's a place you drive through,
put your foot down at the outer edge.
A town that's suspicious of strangers.

This town says *don't get above yourself.*
Don't paint your house
anything more than drabness allows.
In the field beside a repainted cottage
the newcomers planted a citrus orchard.
One night before harvest, someone
stole all the oranges.

The paddocks of caulies and pumpkins
have gone; paspalum and clover
have claimed the rich soil.
But the river will always be there,
thin as a starved snake   waiting
for the deluge to fill its belly.

The bushman's carnival

The crowds have gone.
Come back in the morning, you'll get your winnings
he said to the twelve-year-old boy
from a beachside suburb who, until then,
had never been close enough to rub his hands
over the warm side of a steer.

The dirt is littered with cigarette butts
and paper, but the boy walks on air.
He'd lined up to have a go, to stay
the distance gripping the halter
astride the foaming flanks.

He held on, too terrified to fall.
His head spun. He tasted blood
but was still there
when the bell sounded and they lifted him off.
The tent rodeo had gone by morning
when he'd arrived to collect his money.

She photographs the drought

Influenced by an episode of *Landline* on ABC television

Three roos and a struggling gum
silhouetted on a ridge.
The curious kelpie, paws on the fence, keen eyes,
dusty nose poking through the rails.
The long tongue of a Brahman cow, licking
the crown of her calf. She points her camera
up to the galahs on a lifeless branch.
The sky so pure, so blue, so empty;
the birds, perfectly pink.
The calligraphy of dead limbs,
dissecting the sunset like a church window.

On a dusty track rests a grey bull,
paddocks on either side disappear in a lifeless smudge.
She positions the horizon in her view finder
to best depict the emptiness. The last of her stock sold
after battling the drought for five years.
She's not giving up; she's giving in to a smaller place,
giving in for water.
She points her lens towards the truck,
to the loading of her breeders. She clicks
as the wheels disappear in a haze beyond the gate.

There's still beauty here in this skeletal land;
to prove it she aims and shoots colour –
pegs on a line, a bush burgeoning
with budgerigars, the cattle's water trough filled
with five working dogs cooling off.
She captures the shining orb
of a horse's eye beneath the brush of lashes.
Deep down, life is in limbo. A few fat drops in a dip,
germinate a seed. She zooms in.

*

Each morning shimmers and dusk is blessed
by an intense spectrum of colour.
You let your camera devour this landscape;
the purple shade, the orange light.
You take what you love inside. You're alive
in the midst of death.
Through your lens, it's never looked lovelier.

Van Gogh paints a starry night in Australia

From a painting by Arthur Boyd – *Horse skull under a blanket and a starry night*, 1981

How desolate can a place be?
The stars make his eyes spin.
It's cold – cold enough
to throw a blanket over a dead horse.

The space, all this space, the blue-blackness
seeping into his marrow. Silence
marks the edge of sight.
The pulse of the earth has slowed.
Will night peel from the canvas of the land?

A pallet of blues and purples,
he begins with the constancy of the stars;
his practised hand, swirling paint into diamonds,
drags the sky with his brush.

Instead of cobblestones and shadows,
he smears umber across the surface,
adding decomposition for the smell of death.

A lake of blue mist rests in the lap
of the low range. Nerves flicker
like the white moths around his lantern.
His hand is flying.
He paints a fading comet, scumbles the ridge.

This is earth before its greening, before man
stumbles into the frame.
If he could walk through the low fog, beyond the hills
into the dull haze of magenta, maybe, just maybe,
he'd see the world being born.

Imagine a city

After Italo Calvino, *Invisible Cities*, Vintage Books, London, and
James Gleeson, *Signals from the Perimeter*, Exhibition Catalogue, 1993

1. The City in the Surface

The patterned face of the soil
chains you to the surface.
Scratch your name.
Touch the texture. Chart the craters.
Count the contours.
Trace the wizen imagery of the land.
Stay, until you can no longer read the city
with your fingers.

2. The city of Words

Hold your ear to the page to hear
the struggle between the lines.

3. The City of Brushstrokes

The walls of houses are thick with paint.
Deeds of the past are written in ink
to remain visible.
Every owner who repaints
protects the images of previous owners
who have written their history on walls
since paper became obsolete.
This is just as well as the lies we tell
each other could become fact
were it not for the secret world of art.

4. The Underground City

Spin the tap to open the seal,
let the night flood in.
To dwell in this city, blindfold yourself,
run your palms over every surface,
walk barefoot, feel the textures –
stone, steel, soil. Take that memory
through dark passages.
When it's night, look up –
the light of stars
is almost obscured
by space junk hurtling
through viscous air.
In the penumbra,
the faint edge of reality is receding.
Living beneath the ground,
this claustrophobic existence
is the only safe option.

5. The City of Disappointment

Visit this city on a sunny day.
It rises beyond the range.
Every crystal facet gleams,
reflecting back your vision
of pleasure. The path is paved
with opportunities.
On reaching the city
it fractures into shards.
It's a city you return to
over and over
but never enter.

6. The City of Dreams

Stand up; let your arms sprout,
your feet find crevices.
Let the bark of your body change
with the seasons.

7. The City of Forests

It is three days walk uphill in the fog.
When the echo of a sigh falls upon you,
descend, take nothing with you.
The sky and the light will turn green.
Tread lightly, the forest has ears.
The track twists and turns in on itself.
Lichen's lush growth clings to one side
while the other tumbles
into the sound of water. Old trees have fallen
across the path. Their surface is alive.
Giants grow from the valley floor,
canopies interwoven. Long scarves of moss
hang from branches. The vegetation
is dense and seductive. People who cross the river
never return, though they are not held
against their will. They say, if you cup your hand
and drink the sweet water, you belong
to the forest. The faith that this will last
is held in the heart.
This city, always in cloud, drips light.

The horse in the jungle

Wielding a machete he slashes
leaves, the size of a human,
that droop across the track.
Trudging in fetid air, the sunless,
steamy jungle absorbs us,
and there in the gloom,
nose to a tree-trunk,
a horse, so still it startles me.

Its dark coat is cast in shadow,
head droops as if in prayer,
back hoof angled.
Its ears didn't twitch at our passing.
How out of place
among the birds, butterflies,
bromeliads and fungi.
The air is sticky, thick as honey.

We tower above a silent army –
one that doesn't tremble the earth
or plunder the land.
Marching single file,
each has hoisted a green leaf
cut to identical shape –
upright, little flags disappear
into the undergrowth.

We listen to the hum of insects,
to the jungle whispering.
Stand too long, we will shoot roots,
leaves from our fingers and vines
from our heads curling upwards
towards the light.

The city of sleep

Inspired by James Gleeson, *Signals from the Perimeter,* Exhibition Catalogue, 1993

The stain on the wall
morphs to a restless journey,
dreams itself into our subconscious.
Charcoal cloud fingers – a storm
creeps over as we set out into night
to reach the unknown.

*

I dream the boat has sunk and I'm adrift on a raft.
The waves are rough, not like our beach holidays.

You float down a corridor holding the hand
of a stranger. The days and months fly from you,

and you've passed the burden of life to the ones
left behind. All we can do is watch you go.

How long before the last vestige of memory is gone?
You disappear, and I ache for what is lost.

*

He steps through the ink and the smoke
tattooed all over with a fine needle.
Lines follow the contours of muscle,
the ridge of bone. Flesh tells its story.
The skin is a fine fabric for a machinist.
Intricate pointillist dots mark a life's passage –
dream a name and it will be there.

*

This is the resting place of the night-moth
where your inner compass will guide you.
Here the opal is colourless.
Days and nights are not measured in time
but flit between moments, open into dark vistas
of imagination. Dreams – a collage of memories,
the sweep of a brush in ink and you, a passenger
in the vastness of the mind.
This city disappears when you wake.

Dutch Elm on the Canal du Midi

Each reach is a lung where light
trembles on the speckled trunks.
Our motors resonate
along the ribs of plane trees.
Boughs on both banks arch a canopy
of leaves. The ghosts of themselves
reflect their green and gold shimmer.
How long will they survive?

In the drift and tug of time
the fungus is wreaking havoc.
Carried in the wood of ammunition boxes
by unwitting GIs, it's waterborne,
seeps into the wounds
rubbed raw by mooring lines.
A pink splash of paint marks,
like some outcast, the next to fall.

We steer around the bend
into the pungent odour of oil.
Trees are missing like extracted teeth.
Bonfires in fields – steel jaws
clutch mouthfuls of dead wood
and swing them onto the flames.
In a landscape of loss, under a fierce sun,
the light is brilliant.

Going to the island

Going to the island there's no train or bridge.
Be it a dream or a boat setting out
to slice through the morning fog.
No passport or ticket needed, pay the ferryman
for the one hour journey. High tide
the red and green channel markers are winking.

At the wharf there's a café on wheels, blue umbrellas.
A warm breeze waves the mist away.
I would sip hot coffee near the ramp
where we launched our tinny in all weathers.
Unassailed by tyres mushrooms grow
on the steep, dirt road.

The stars sing the sad story
over the house where a young girl died,
but only I know the tune,
and the boy who went wild with grief has gone.

There's the crumbling hideaway
with a wall made from coloured bottles
that shimmered light over the wooden floor
where an old piano was smashed to fingerlings.
Not a sound to tremble the dogs' ears.
On a quiet night, a stubbie in their hands,
they tell the story of the spectre that roamed inside.

As it was demolished
snakes like twisted branches dropped
into the dozer's cabin.
A python hunting possums
fell through the ceiling and was shot,
hung in the poinsettia.

It's a prediction of rain when ants grow wings
and swarm from stumps, when hairy huntsmen
hide behind cupboards.
There's a poem in the iridescent green clouds
sailing in from the west, hail hammering the tin roof,
bruising the mangos.

Water tanks bulged,
the dirt roads became rivers,
a chorus of frogs and toads rejoiced for days,
ferns lunged over paths and each other. Worms
contorted in the saturated air.

We sat on verandas,
filled baths, tramped mud inside,
partied to welcome the washing of trees.
Some friends thought us crazy living here.
It seeped into our bones – the swamps,
each sandy track, the smooth limbs of the mangroves,
the hair-raising scream of the bush stone-curlew.

The place I came from remains a dull ache. There's more
than enough of it behind the eyes, more than enough
to fill me for a lifetime.

Go to Tokyo

for *chadō* and the grace in the hands of the tea master,
for the joy of seeing snow-capped Mt Fuji
        through graffiti-free train windows,
to know the kindness of a stranger who found the hotel
        while the wheelchair he pushed was parked at the corner,
to wander clean streets or take taxis, their seats
        covered in white, crocheted seat covers,
        clean and neat as grandma's best tablecloth,
to watch people cycling to work in the rain
        sitting up as straight as Mary Poppins
        holding their see-through umbrellas,
for the patience of the waiter searching the food section
        in a translation book,
to board the *shinkansen* in queues
        calm and orderly as the herd
        filing through a gate,
for peace and conformity
        and the man on the train who sleeps, his head
        on a tourist's shoulder,
to visit arcades where florists leave their flowers
        out overnight, and they're still there
        in the morning, brimming with promise,
to know with certainty French pastries and good coffee
        await in the basement of Mitsukoshi department store,

to step up from the underground
        where everyone is rushing in all directions,
for the joy of walking in a crowded market
        slurping pineapple on sticks,
for the gardener on his knees cutting grass with shears,
to join people wafting smoke over their faces,
        burning away impurities,
to happen upon a building site where men wear white
        gloves while mixing concrete,
to marvel at plastic food shiny as polished shoes
        in the windows of restaurants,
for the transience of *sakura* and the joy in its celebration,
to fall into bed at night,
to do it all again tomorrow.

chadō – the tea ceremony
sakura – cherry blossom

Minutiae

Last year has spun into space
orbiting with all the other debris
encompassing
all we did,
all we were.
The grind of each day gone
like a forgotten memory,
unaccountable,
even the smallest scrap.
Thoughts, lost emails,
discarded poems,
gestures tiny enough to pierce
the visor of a space walker,
promises thin as gold leaf
circling the earth
at eight kilometres per second
among
one hundred million fragments
of minute matter.

Autumn's Passage

old temple
a butterfly rests
on the closed door

Autumn riot

They come like a hot torch of colour –
the air thick – a riot of screeching.
Red and green parrots

among the thick branches
and the ripe fruit. Exhilaration
pumps the sky blue.

The tree is shaking; it seems so happy.
I swear it shakes with mirth.
Its fat-belly is alive with shrieks.

In the deepness of autumn,
the apple tree radiates its abundance,
and the birds know exactly where to go.

A place called somewhere

It's somewhere she says.
Somewhere – a secret kept by birds.
The giddy tumble of confusion
finding her handbag under the towels,
prescriptions stolen by intruders.
What size is somewhere?
It's as large as a suitcase someone stole,
or as big as a missing shoe, heavy
as a full set of stoneware plates. We think
it's with her umbrella and dressing gown
though she denies this and claims
it is definitely in her mother's house
curled up like a mouse in its hole.
The vacuum cleaner lead has disappeared
behind the bookcase or morphed into a shoebox.
What shape is somewhere? Thin like glass
on the top shelf or the TV's missing remote.
It's the negative space between tea pots and jugs,
among sunbeams and dust motes.
It's floating or hovering on wings.
Where is this place called somewhere?
When the sun appears
the birds can't keep her secret.

The music of snow

I would like to tell you
about music that falls like snow
in the warm rooms of our house.
Snow that falls like music
over hills beyond the window.
The velvety, black cat slinking
down the garden steps,
concealed in shadow.
The bushes that drip melted snow.
The old willow's yellow filigree
beneath a charcoal sky.
In green water goldfish glide through
concentric circles, succumbing
to a patch of sunlight.
A noisy family of butcher birds
circles the pond.

I need to tell you how music
no longer falls in my mother's house.
How the snow is filling her mind,
how it keeps on falling.
The whiteness of loss
that will one day soon, leave her
a pristine expanse of snow.

Living in the cracks

after Jane Smith
        after Laurie Duggan

I'm starting to imagine my mother's
life is taking a different course.
Was it her or me that lost the car
in the underground car park? She tells the story.
I am her daughter, is she my child?
Memory unravelling when she tries to recall
the restaurant's name, or the street it's on.
The car wash – she was supposed to remember
how to get there, to wind the windows up.
I'm living in the cracks between two lives
can't bring myself to say she should be assessed.
The missing house keys are found in the grass.
I miss the exit thinking of her and go around again.
Waking to a new day when the earth wobbles.

I'm starting to imagine my mother's
in the underground car park. She tells the story,
the restaurant's name, or the street it's on.
I'm living in the cracks between two lives.
I miss the exit thinking of her and go around again.
Life is taking a different course
I am her daughter, is she my child?
The car wash – she was supposed to remember,
can't bring myself to say she should be assessed.
Waking to a new day when the earth wobbles.
Was it her or me that lost the car?
Memory unravelling when she tries to recall
how to get there, to wind the windows up.
The missing house keys are found in the grass.

I'm starting to imagine my mother's
waking to a new day when the earth wobbles.
Life is taking a different course,
I miss the exit thinking of her and go around again.
Was it her or me that lost the car?
The missing house keys are found in the grass.
In the underground car park she tells the story,
can't bring myself to say she should be assessed,
I am her daughter, is she my child?
I'm living in the cracks between two lives.
Memory unravelling when she tries to recall
how to get there, to wind the windows up,
the restaurant's name, or the street it's on.
The car wash – she was supposed to remember.

I'm starting to imagine my mother's
memory unravelling when she tries to recall.
Can't bring myself to say she should be assessed.
Life is taking a different course –
the restaurant's name, or the street it's on,
the missing house keys are found in the grass.
Was it her or me that lost the car?
The car wash – she was supposed to remember.
I miss the exit thinking of her and go around again
in the underground car park. She tells the story –
how to get there, to wind the windows up.
Waking to a new day when the earth wobbles,
I am her daughter, is she my child?
I'm living in the cracks between two lives.

The journey

I lead her by the hand
down an unknown road
and into a foreign country
where I must learn the language.

Outside I brim confidence.
Inside I tremble,
unsure as to what awaits us. She trusts me
and comes willingly.
With our travel agent's help
our itinerary is mapped out –
we've a mountain
of paper to climb
places to visit, people to see,
help along the way.
A train ride or a bus trip
to manicured gardens,
the meals will be tasty,
a comfortable bed each night.

This is our journey. She wears a smile,
a pale pink cardigan over a floral blouse,
a silk scarf held in place with a butterfly brooch.
My mother has dementia
and I've never seen her look more beautiful.

A lasting memory

In memory of Pauline T.

When I recall our visit to Istanbul
it is not the sheets of rain soaking the four us
as we paid the inflated price for umbrellas
or the taxi driver who fleeced and dropped us
a long way from our destination

although it should be the view
from the breakfast room of our boutique hotel –
the dome and minarets
of the Blue Mosque one side
and the ancient Hagia Sophia on the other

and when I hold my hand-painted bowls
with their riotous colour,
it's not the market I recall – but you –
as we walked down the cobblestone street
in search of a recommended restaurant,

how you hung back,
perhaps you preferred to be alone,
and I was afraid you'd get lost in the crowd,
or your balance would let you down
on the uneven surface, so I turned
and saw

how lightly you stepped, how straight your back,
your face tilted, laughing
with the handsome young man beside you;
the young girl in you flirting
as if Alzheimer's had flown.

Dinner for six

Swap the contents
        of the kitchen drawers around.

            Take all the food
      from the freezer.

Defrost it
        on the windowsill.

Fill saucepans with carrots
        potatoes and peas.

Stash them in the fridge.

Don't mention
        the word dementia.

From your lips
            it's an omen.

            Chain it under the sink.

Set the table, feed guests

            who never arrive.

There's someone else living here

You want to go home now
to the place over there –
indicated by a wave of your hand.
This is not your kitchen, your crockery;
you can't find a teaspoon to stir coffee;
a strange pink kettle has settled on the bench.

It has come to this – my mother,
who rode horses,
walked in the Himalayas,
climbed the slippery slope of a volcano
and danced the reel
circles the vinyl on unsteady legs.

There've been many kitchens.
Her late husband's importunity unsettled her;
boxes packed then unpacked somewhere new:
Many memories to fall back on
now new ones no longer configure.

You tell me there is someone else living here
someone who walks behind you,
moves things to confuse.
Staring out the kitchen window
you say you want to go home,
then in the paddock behind the fence
the white horses walk past
and you know where you are.

Combined Assets and Income Assessment

How much is my house worth?
How can I tell you
of bricks and mortar when I want you to know
about the rhododendrons I planted, their mauves, pinks
and reds, of the sunlight that warms a cold room
and the fire that blazes on a winter's day.

You want to know if I have any life insurance policies,
and I recall how I walked in the Himalayas, twice.

You ask am I a veteran. I looked that up –
a person or thing that has given long service
in some capacity.
To that I answer yes.

Am I married? Where can I write
of the car accident on a mountain road
that took his life and nearly mine.

You want me to attach a document when I want to attach
a picture of my four children.

How much money do I have?
Perhaps you should ask this after I buy a room in the nursing home.

What is the net value of my household contents?
Do you want to know the value of the vase
my brother bought for me in Venice
or my grandmother's silver tea pot, perhaps the rugs
from Tibet I've walked on every day for forty years.

How old is my house?
My house is a lot younger than me
and it carries itself well. If it was a woman
it would be in its prime.

Is there anything that may affect the value of my home?
Do I have any income stream products?
Perhaps I can answer both those questions together:
I have an incoming stream through my garden
every time the lettuce farm siphons off its overflow.

What is the value of my car? The value is immeasurable.
We travel everywhere together
and I've never looked under the bonnet.

No I don't have bonds or debentures; however,
I do have dentures.

Please attach proof of all account balances.
My accounts never balance.

You want to know
how many properties I own so I'll tell you
I have snippets in my heart of each of my homes,
enough for a mansion on a hill and a river below.
I'm not sure which one I live in.

Small poems of loss for my mother

coming home
without her　　how hollow
the clouds

*

her driveway empty
except for shadows

*

stepping into rain
　　　　without her umbrella

*

a shell to my ear
listening
for my mother's voice

Weaving life into a day

Sunset blinks through broken blades
I hold her hand as I did my child's
The scar from the scissors
Under my palm
Drivers wait patiently
The flower-painted walking stick
Hides in the dark cupboard
She says, *look at the mountain*
I walked up there last week
It's twelve months since the fire
Now there's more green than black
More shedding of brain pathways
I'm 88, my brain is too full
I'm making room
Stewed fruit and jelly on Fridays
A hollowed out tooth
Anaesthesia looms
Her clothes are packed in plastic bags
Waiting for the word home
Learn to soothe
Kind lies flow from my mouth
My mother's reality can't be fathomed
I'm forever dog-paddling
In her deep water
A black dog muscles into our yard
Chasing the pademelon
I'm not in control
Weaving life into the day's mystery

Looking after chickens

At the home's entrance
>	cracks
>	in the earth widen. Inside
music whispers
>	to memory
>	reducing the frequency
to wander,
>	help tolerate stress.

Dinnertime can be chaotic.
>	You are marooned
when your tide comes in.

You tremble,
>	cut your finger
on a tinge of yellow light,   dreams
>	shatter in glass.

You're static,
>	fixed to a leaf with special glue
while outside
>	the garden swarms with birds.

Twisting hands,
>	counting fingernails,
you search
>	the corridors
>	for familiar faces.

You said you always loved
                the bad boys,
that's why you're here –
                to look after chickens.

A splinter of light

Her head
is full of cobwebs;
the kind that mesh the gaps
between trees
and tangle a bird
in full flight.
If she could be
that bird
for three heartbeats,
her quick brain focused on
the weakest weave,
wings pressed to ribs,
she'd pass through
beak piercing a hole
to the sky, darting
into a prism of light.
Still her heart,
stop the blood, the breath.
She's free.
A splinter of light, three beats
from a needle's point, a beak
snaring light.
Three beats between
life and death.

The dark disturbance

Aching for home she stands in her room
staring at the window. How long has she been here?
She's not sure where she lives,
what house she owns, or how many.

A landscape opens up; her grandmother's house,
a Chinese market garden near the river.
She has the feeling she lives there.
All these houses are reminders of loss.

A pregnant possum catches her eye, scampering
back and forth over fresh pine bark,
pink nose twitching, frantic for the dark space
beneath the building to give birth.

Is it autumn? The gardener has cleared leaves,
cut back, cleaned the fish pond, blocked the hole.
She turns from her cloud of confusion,
trembling like a moth against glass.

The uncertainty of her plans drift like mist.
Plastic bags are packed with clothes;
her longing, at times more than she can bear.
If only she could remember where she lives.

The egret on the edge

One leg anchored in mud
the other warmed in feathers.
The egret on the edge
of shadow
hunches into itself.
Below, the dark swamp is teaming.
Light hovers on a leaf,
a feather
and creeps imperceptibly
towards night.

Above the lake

In a rising mist
blurring the edge of reality
a bird curves

wings stretching
the lightness of bone
seem no heavier

than a feather
falling
the only movement

to hover
on the bleary edge
of morning.

About the author

Lorraine Haig moved to Tasmania from Queensland in the early 1990s. She has a fine arts degree from UTAS. Her poetry book *An Ocean of Sky* was published in 2014 by Burringbah Books.

Her haiku have been published in print and online journals here and around the world, including *Communion Arts Journal*, December 2018; *Rengay by two poets*, Red Moon Press Anthology 2018; *Still Heading Out* – an anthology of Australian and New Zealand haiku; *Presence* UK; *Windfall*; *Wales Haiku Journal*; and *Blue Giraffe*.

Some of her longer poems have been published in anthologies and journals in Australia, including *Australian Poetry Journal, Blue Giraffe, Famous Reporter, Poetrix, Poetry d'Amour, The Gallipoli Poetry Project* 2014, and the anthology *The Persistence of Song*. She was invited to respond to a painting for the first edition of the online magazine *Islet*.

www.ingramcontent.com/pod-product-compliance
Lightning Source LLC
Chambersburg PA
CBHW070939080526
44589CB00013B/1571